FOREST BOOKS

ROOM WITHOUT WALLS

BO CARPELAN is one of the leading Finnish poets writing in Finland-Swedish. Born in 1926, he is the son of a bank clerk. His first book of poems appeared in 1946 and he received his doctorate in 1960. Since then he has written 14 volumes of verse and is also a novelist, playwright, essayist and critic.

He also writes for children. His works have been translated into Finnish, Danish, Norwegian, German, English, Polish, Slovak and French, but this is the first full book-length edition of Carpelan's poetry in English. Among other distinctions, in 1980 he was awarded a five-year professorship by the Finnish State Committee for Literature.

ANNE BORN is well known as a fine translator, writer and poet. She received her M.A. in English language and literature at the University of Copenhagen and a B. Litt at Oxford. Her sensitive renderings of Carpelan's poems have been published previously in magazines and reviews.

HANNU TAINA is a well known and distinguished Finnish artist who illustrated Bo Carpelan's *The Courtyard (Gården)* in the Finnish edition.

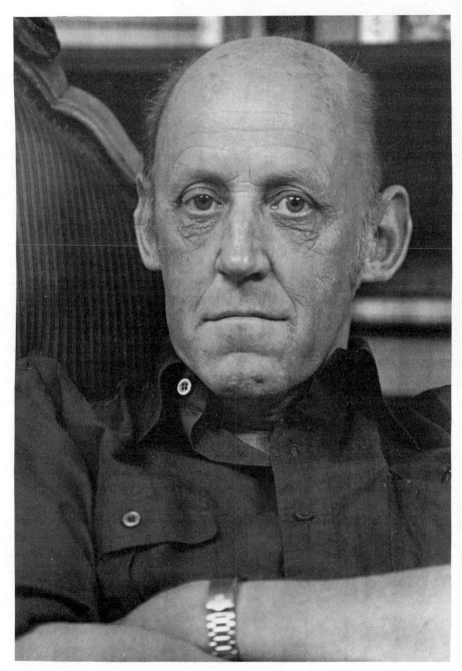

Bo Carpelan

ROOM WITHOUT WALLS

SELECTED POEMS
by

BO CARPELAN

Translated by
ANNE BORN

Illustrated by
HANNU TAINA

FOREST BOOKS
LONDON ☆ 1987 ☆ BOSTON

PUBLISHED BY FOREST BOOKS
20 Forest View, Chingford, London E4 7AY, U.K.
61 Lincoln Road, Wayland, M.A. 01788, U.S.A.

First published 1987

Typeset in Great Britain by Cover to Cover, Cambridge
Printed in Great Britain by A. Wheaton & Co. Ltd, Exeter

British Library Cataloguing in Publication Data
Carpelan, Bo
Room without walls: selected poems
I. Title   II. Born, Anne
839.7'174   PT 9875. C35
ISBN 0–948259–08–6

Library of Congress Catalogue Card No
87–080139

The paintings of Hannu Taina were originally created
for Bo Carpelan's collection *The Courtyard (Gården)*,
recently republished in hard-back edition,
Bonniers, Sweden (1985).

Cover graphics by Ann Evans

Contents

7

All poems, except those from THE DAY IS TURNING, also appear in the selection POEMS OF THIRTY YEARS (1980).

Introduction

Finland, the Nordic country furthest from Britain, has, like Canada, a dual-language culture. Finnish belongs to the Finno-Ugrian family of languages which includes Finnish, Hungarian and some ten languages spoken in the Soviet Union, and is completely different from the Scandinavian languages. But because Finland was part of Sweden for six centuries, Swedish was the language of officialdom and most literature until the second half of the nineteenth century; the variant spoken and written in Finland is now termed Finland-Swedish. As well as folk poetry in Finnish, from which the epic *Kalevala* was compiled, over the past century literature has grown and flourished in Finland-Swedish; and the late 20th century sees a flowering of every genre.

A number of Finnish poets took part in a Finnish festival at the Poetry Society London in October 1985. Bo Carpelan was among them. Perhaps the greatest poet writing in Finland today, born in 1926, he has also read with success in America. Since his first volume in 1946 Carpelan has published a dozen collections and *Selected Poems of Thirty Years* in 1980. He has written short stories, novels, a thriller, children's books, and worked for radio and television.

A number of Carpelan's poems have been published in translation in magazines and anthologies, but this is his first full collection in English. Although he acknowledges early influences from Georg Trakl, the French writers Jacob and Elouard, and above all Wallace Stevens, Bo Carpelan's poetry is uniquely original. Like the Faroese poet William Heinesen, Carpelan takes much inspiration from nature, its stern northern wintry presence and delicate spring and summer aspects. For him nature is a metaphor for language, is itself language. In an essay,

9

November Credo, published in an English translation in *Swedish Book Review*, May 1984, Carpelan described what this meant in the context of his writing: 'The landscape: a vast room. This language room exists within each one of us, unexpressed to a higher and lesser degree.' He believes writing, reading, the use of language is a vital part of life. In an interview he said: 'Poor language means poor experience and this leads to trouble in the psychological sense and to many people in mental hospitals. It is a tragedy for a human being when he cannot use language.'

There is a landscape of the world, of one's own place, of one's life, one's time, one's death, one's mind and imagination. In Carpelan's poems all these interchange, aware of each other in a mystical communion. In style concise, pure and clear, in form economical, he writes with a delicate lyrical beauty of fundamental human experience. Beneath the spare, deceptively simple surface lie vast eternities, gentle echoes, mysteries, sorrows, signs and warnings.

Many poems are set in the natural world. Many others are interiors, whether as in 'On contemplating some old Flemish masters', they regard the significances of those apparently clear-cut rooms, or recall the tensions and feelings of childhood homes as in the sequence 'The Courtyard'.

In Bo Carpelan's world the ordinary course of daily life in its simplicity, peace, tragedy and blessing is as resonant as the cosmos. The old woman on the shore bent over a bucket is archetypal, depicted with the least elaboration.

Anne Born

from
Like a Dusky Warmth
(1946)

Lyric sequence

1 This unending line:
cheek, throat, road, horizon;
a sleeper, poised between death
and life, tender closed eyelids
Joy in light steps,
sun, wet leaves and space
and all old well-springs' song of time,
the beauty of summer, gentle paths
and little bitter herbs.
Shadows playing on a resting hand
and a day of heat, trees and swallows.
This unending line:
cheek, throat, road, horizon.

2 Now the quick shadows die
in a pensive yearning. Parting
fills the air early with age.
The invisible path is far too close,
the hand's rest broken.
A song grows in the sun's vacuum,
tells of the last shadow's silent course.

3 Beyond the fields' solitude, dark shores
beyond the fields' fire, hills and wind.
Darkness erupts from deep wells
cool as all that's utmost in the hour
and behind lattices a door
slams out startled hoof-beats –
By dark waters, burned out,
hear, this storm from the cathedral's mantle,
this song and cleft of silence.

4 Now all memories fade
the hand grasps no stars –
sorrows, cradlesongs and early dawn:
a space of loss
a space of shadows' empty play.

Like a dusky warmth

In the fleece of evening
someone passes with a lantern,
the pendulum's secret hope
like a dusky warmth
towards dawn.

Morning

Shore, sky not a shadow moving
here the hand's distance blossoms
grass silver-clear –
O quiet hush
      All is close to dream.

Quiet time

A woodcock stumps along.
Sunbaked clay makes room for hidden springs,
the sunlight reaches its own meaning.
I stand barefoot in eternally
soft and water-drunk moss, see
the light and shade of leaf-play in my heart,
the calm chill of silence in my blood.

Songs of the shadow

The shadow's hidden
in the lover's glance;
the hours bloom, close
their petals.
When all shores lie quiet
the shadow drinks the heart's
last dream.

In the swift twilight
where branches now lie
like faint brush-strokes
the shadow wonders at
the swallows' sleep;
as the lone man passes
the shadow stalks his vacant steps.

from
You Dark Survivor
(1947)

Sea

Here's where I've come to. Here a boundary
parts earth and sea: wave against wave,
gale against a silence red as jelly-fish.
A moon-road leads across the dark. Quietly
traces of grief and tedium fade out into the sand.
Here a swallow has cut through evening's net.
Here the fire burns clearest, quenched by waves
to chillness. A mirrored silence,
a film of water-dreams, song
for a stranger, sap for an ageing oak.
Here's where I've come to. A sea, a leave-taking
for the dark. A boundary between silence
and secrecy. Wave-forests, burned caravels,
eyes and eye-sockets turned towards drifting stars.

August

Who weaves at your dusky loom, August
whose hand guides the shuttle through all shadows
melting into each other, blotted out,

your singular web of life and coming death
that dream you conjure with your hair,
                    your lips
the quiet rain of slaked stars that will force

all whispers from the maple's roving hands
on to frost and loneliness, tell me, who
has woven quiet ruin into your glow?

from
Minus Seven
(1952)

Birth

When I was born I went back to a world I felt I knew better than my father and mother did. Their first conversation with me seemed alien; leaning over me they plunged my gaze in shadow; I slept, dreaming I was a little child. Was I changed in the dream? I woke crying.

Night at the opera

As soon as the performance began my mother broke in to back up my sister, who was then a mere extra in the crowd scenes. Armed only with high spirits, after quite a struggle she made her way on to the stage and during an interval in the music before the hero came on, she began to sing a little song, while my sister, wild with joy, sobbed in the dusty wings. The audience fell into step with the tune at once and joined in my mother's song with gusto. The whole Opera House resounded with a great surge of music, and I alone of the family kept my presence of mind. In the end the atmosphere began to overwhelm me and I made for the exit. When I cautiously looked down from the doors at the world below me I saw how the whole Opera House was gently swinging to and fro, like a drunken shining glass ball hung from a thread, formed of my sister's sobs, the only sound to reach me from where I stood. I had to struggle not to burst into tears.

The continual reunion

You stop. At the same moment a bird disappears into a tree. Our paths have changed but little, even after your death. The same wind, the same bird, the same tree. And yet the memory suddenly bows me down, in sharp pain.

The water-colour

After I had gone over the tree with a brush, quickly dipped in water, it began to fade gently. While there was still time I shaded in the sky with a dark blue that spread, deepened and immersed my room in softly falling darkness; high in the air above I drew a black streak; afterwards my room rested in nocturnal silence, my hand no longer saw the finished water-colour which surrounded me with its scent of water and trees. Next morning the landscape had dried; when I looked out of the window I saw space and foliage, cool and still.

Our housekeeper

Our housekeeper was a heavy-featured woman. Her total lack of beauty was single-minded and severe. She was always silent and brooding; only her eyes reflected something – we did not understand it. One day she disappeared from our town. We took it she had gone back to her own village and one fine Sunday we decided to combine business with pleasure: get some fresh air and pay the strange woman the money owed her. We came to a place whose very name seemed brimming with freshness. We rested on grass cool as water, towards evening we listened to distant cries from people homeward-bound. We made our way slowly back to the station, given over to silence.

The smell of snow

The smell of snow, like clean glass, is so faint that only a written reflection on it can give any idea of its almost non-existent nature.

The monkey

With its silver-plated chain like a hissing snake behind it, the trained monkey creeps to and fro in front of the massive bookcase. I watch its master: he leans back in his chair, watching the smoke from his cigarette softly disperse and die away, talking of war and the unbearable lot of humanity. And I? I look at my hands, remembering poverty I could wish on no one. The regular sound of the monkey's chain swells to a roar that blots out my eyes, drowns all beauty in a surge of youth, shame and memories.

The nanny

She has wrinkled speckled hands. When I greet her she giggles and makes a low curtsey. She shakes her memories round in her head, big as a clenched fist. She lies in a basket chair clutching a photograph of me as a child. When I say goodbye, with an effort she heaves herself up, lost in memories.

Sunday

I have turned round in my chair to observe my eyes. The room has shifted; whose face am I turning? It rains and rains; wind and scent of water reach me through the open window. Now I see: it was the sky I was looking at. The heavens! The rain slackens, the window closes, I rest my head in my hands and am borne away by the swift darkness.

Loneliness

If I'd not been so lonely I would never have endured this lack of human beings.

from
Object for Word
(1954)

Horses

Horses, vanishing wildly in a cloud of dust,
Here on the verandah my heart still beats
with the flying echo of hooves:
red whirls through the dusk.

On contemplating some
old Flemish masters

1

The perspective's well-known. We stroll through the room.
The landscape's changed, a mere part of life.
We sense it, unseen; so, it overshadows us.
Our blood adjusts to it, moves in utter silence,
perfects our outward likeness in an inner reality.

2

She is conscious of the agonies ahead.
But in her white ruffled collar still keeps calm.
Her childlike hands rest too, and their pose touches us
where we hide ourselves in detail, recalls us to
our childhood, to the future, like the master unknown.

3

The one and only needful sign of love:
the closeness of wife's and husband's hands. Between them,
the flower vase with its reflection from an unseen window,
and the grey background, life's tapestry: the background
for our returns those they quietly regard with their meek eyes.

4

The evening falls silent, birds hush. Turned away
in towards his room he hears our steps
as if already stilled, stumbling over his courtyard;
a turmoil, alien to the muted colours in his hand.

Elegy

Your hair's a star-cluster I saw transformed.
It lives, bleeds like a hurt creature
on the earth's field, in my inmost dream.
It cuts the dark into stones and geometry there.
No winds touch you; you yourself rest
under sand, silvered with sand. Darkness
falls and strikes me in my sleep; I half-turn
on my side, embrace a corpse.
The wind from the sea props itself on its elbow,
pierces my breast, echoes with slack hands.
No river of blessing-bearing water
binds the hearts of stars and humans now.
I see how the soul, freed, once searched
on wings for a limited, limitless space.
There your blood spread like frozen spray
                    in the dark's foam,
changed into a constellation round your death.
                    Asbestos-clad
your rocket-like late sister finds her dead reflection.
Your hair's a star-cluster I saw transformed,
on a night when the heart tugs uneasily at its bonds
under the starry sky's leaking jetties, under
                    crumbling walls.

from
The Landscape's Transformations
(1957)

At Grand Opera

Through the ox-eye the drama's mere pantomime
here in the gods at the opera house where passion flares:
far down in the earth's stalls the audience sits
stiff as silver foil in a smoke of voices.

The bloodshot eye sees in a world-stage action
only this unheard voice from the grave of grimaces
that climbs to us near the space-roof's smooth arch
to hear what we couldn't hear from unknown agony,

and to waver in wind-currents no-one has felt
except one giddily watching who sees his life
realised at a distance, near the abyss
and hear's humanity's voice like a glissando in darkness.

Soft music.

'Soft music like quiet talk,'
snow whirling through the window
and the silence after a meal;
bread broken and blood
formed like a ring of fire
through the paths in an eye
turned inward to the universe.

Alien

You're someone else in this city.
Avenues with leaves of frost
and time,
far beyond life's stone-paved streets.
Your youth, footsteps,
you see it all in memory,
beast-like, poised to spring
under autumn's crowns.

Shrink the world

On the mountain, our mountain
stands a tree
in shadow, carved from flying sunlight.
A grub sees the tree as a darkness
and no clouds. By its scale
we come no further than dark and light.
Shrink the world!
I want to see darkness on the mountain,
                    the mountain's dark,
darkness of all space and in that dark
the ordinary light, like a flash
and your soul's outline.

Starting point

One who's walked roads, on his own,
hearing, noting those who pass,
is solitary, just solitary,
if a voice, a hand like a firebrand doesn't harass
the quiet hours, a life's defences.
One who's walked roads, alone
and not been abandoned by solitude,
has a starting point.

Quiet evening

No-one comes near.
The room bleeds
like a blossom,
a silenced mouth;

the sleeping child
in the sleeping mother
turns towards
its image in the night;

it's snowing, the wind
sweeps away
the hesitant traces
of my youth.

Words move to
the still centre,
light as mountains
carried by winds.

The landscape's transformations

The landscape's transformations,
the sea's sleep-drunk cry by the bed
where love had already woken –
eternal landscape
like ringing clouds in the wind,
voices before death reaped them,
people, droves of cattle
and the falling night of silence –
the eternal wave's
dark reflections
dazzling through the blood:
wandering through you
I see the shadow-play of loss
and the floating weight of burning mountains.

Evening

Evening with the four trees
and a wind,

with the sisters, cloud in cloud,
drifting over;

the hour when the word,
ground dull, turns

like an oval, a bleeding stone
or a heart

whose boundaries are transformed,
a landscape ever transformed,

yet always the same.

Completed

Bright daylight falling
through the window; autumn
exalts the broad acres.
Then in still splendour
our fields deepen,
birds fly and like spring-water
voices fall through the shimmering airy vault.
Finally, the meeting with silence,
a figure, unmoving, tree-like.

from
The Cool Day
(1960)

Autumn walk

A man walks through the woods
on a day of shifting light.
Meets few people,
stops, observes the autumn sky.
He's making for the churchyard
and no-one's following him.

In the June dawn

In the early June dawn he rowed,
dressed up, choked by a neck-tie, trousers turned up,
across the calm bay, turned, looked back;
there was the island, there slept his wife and child,
trees, the winds rested there,
the first breeze of morning came and broke
the mirrored water.

Morning, evening

Cool, the grass rests,
it is morning, evening
in your life.
Close to your paths
goes the last day
hidden perhaps in the tree's leaves
or in quiet cities
where your cry's unheard.

The mute grass

The heart doesn't agree with its limits,
nor the poem with reality,
nor reality with God's dream.
What kind of a dialogue is it that changes you
yet doesn't change you?
Don't search in the mute grass,
search the mute grass.

Evening

Fleeting dawn, fleeting day, but the cool evening
comes with its twilight, goes like the bay's water
among the dark trees that stand unmoving.
And among waves from endless distance voices reach us,
softly, fragments of words sink through the air –
fleeting, fleeting is our day but evening lingers in
                    a summery warmth;
cool summer's warmth, stay on in the blood
                    which must darken here
under the crowns of trees, under the eye of heaven's
open, boundlessly open gaze.

Old woman and path

A shimmer of light fell over the fields,
we couldn't see its source. Everywhere plains, forests
under the lilac-blue sky. The dead reeds
shone like gold beside the chill water.
On the shore an old woman bent over a bucket,
went off through the woods without seeing us.
Then we continued our journey.
First we learned to follow in the woman's steps,
her path lost itself in the woods.
Later we heard the reeds before the wind reached us.
Lastly we saw the gleam from the sky,
made out the light that comes from darkness
and goes out smiling.

Morning wash

After word on word was spoken everything stayed,
what was touched by winds, sank blood-red
and came again in morning silence before the lowly eye,
to the hedgehog's snout and the shadows.
With life's deftness and flux the poem seeks
dark earth, and in its flight shapes
wholeness. Parts of me rest in my morning
like stones on the shore.
There the one I love does the morning wash,
cleaner than words, with the morning water.
There my son goes walking through my life
and all these images are things, alive,
that have already said about the word
what the word cannot say and what the
              bay says.

In timelessness

The travellers melted into the shadows,
their voices faded and you too
were distanced from yourself,
yet closer, as if words
lingered among trees as tree,
or image of trees.
It was in timelessness
where islands rest on the hand's water-mirror.

And while the silence lasted you heard
the voices of father and mother;
then a bird tuned up
and their voices merged into one voice.
It was the silence when the forest still
graced life with its leaves,
and days gathered.
Brief time we're given.

Premonition

It was summer-time,
a door open to the night breeze.
You'd never followed softer paths
in the dew of morning,
past resting shores.
A cloud came,
someone woke,
you heard beloved voices
and night's shadow, the last one,
touched you.

The early morning

Early morning and early grass,
quiet roads, wide farms and meadows,
familiar shadows, parts of the light
and we share the stillness, the lingering mind.

Through the evening

Bright stars through the evening,
a bird on watch.
Trees move in a child's eyes,
the bird watches on,
till the wind stills.

Simple songs

Simple songs, clear as morning –
how many lives and thoughts have sunk
so these might rise,
grass, flowers, days, passings.

Your figure by the table

Your figure by the table,
the shadow of the child's head on your hand, fruit,
your gaze through the window fixed on the trees'
movements,
the movement reflected in a knife cutting bread,
the use and clarity of things.

The army

Mirrored in a crossed window-pane
the army goes by and disappears
into the city that closes behind it,
into the wound
that never closes.

Broken pattern

Where have you been, you I knew well?
– In a darkness,
vacant, deranged.
There goes one who will be changed
and like dogs
the winds run through his limbs.
You're like him. From you I can expect
nothing
but suffering that is burnt-out happiness
and at the uttermost darkness
happiness that's burnt-out suffering
and breaks the pattern.

Tell me

Tell me before you leave me
if the weariness I felt even at night,
if the world that never sleeps, steps
moving towards the same goal –
tell me before you leave me
if anything has been said or unsaid,
you who know everything and don't answer questions
but move over the fields like a heraldic bird.

Long night

Some day when the boundary between yesterday and
        tomorrow
is a barely-felt change of light
and trees stand guard outside the window,
some evening in your maturity a cold wave washes
slowly through you.
You know nothing about the darkness that has come down;
it's God watching you turning away, in moonlight,
and the life you're living, compared with this night,
        is short.

In another Umbria

In another Umbria, in drifting smoke
the wind reaches you and you see
a clarity, the light. We rest under its vault.
Nothing is strange here where you put
your hand on mine in the springtime field,
in another Umbria, in the shadows.
With purling water the morning
slips unnoticed through the valleys
where other birds sing for one who fell silent,
grief turned to calm,
lasted as the light grew.
The day soon high and the grass by the road tall.

from
The Courtyard
(1969)

The courtyard

The brown tablecloth nearly reached the floor.
I sat beneath it unseen in the scent of
                    cabbage and warmth.

The sky hung on rusty hooks,
                    the courtyard women shrank.
They were the summer's only flowers.
They carried buckets to the inner yard
                    where there was no sun.

Father read the paper, in the desk's middle drawer
were bills, I.O.U.'s, pawn-tickets, rent-book, all in order.

Somewhere behind house on house the sea rocked,
                    like an oil-slick,
you could glimpse it if you leaned out of the attic window.
But it's the kitchen table I remember best,
it wasn't often cleared.

Life, it was a mystery, you had to take care,
go in and out with your skin like a bruise
                    you couldn't touch.
The sky was quite clear above the carpet-beating balcony.

What mattered was earning some money, getting a living.
What mattered was a room, a bed behind the kitchen
and saving for something bigger.

The water in the courtyard well was clear as any spring.

Memory – a blind leap into the future
Where your children grow up.

There wasn't a hope of keeping the window on to
the inner yard clean.
Maybe it was just as well not to have a clear view,
roofs and chimney-pots and even the sky were friendly
when you'd given up like this. When it rained
the water formed streets of little drops, almost silvery.
I watched them closely.
It was beyond me to see what use I could make of them.

The insides of the earphones were quite hot.
They smelt of shellac.
Inside the blind tuner with its crystal
a filament was aimed.
Shrill voices from the ether scattered like iron filings.
Suddenly a clear note spread over the earth's surface.
It was Mozart, of all things, like delicate fumes
from my cigar box.

Even if clothes were hard to come by, the food was always good,
even if money was scarce, necessities were there,
even if the family bookcase was scant there was the library:
a better school than school
where your knees starved and your skin felt too tight.
Even if it was winter there was a Christmas star,
a candle, a glass on the table, two glasses and my face,
and theirs who are dead now.
They lived up to a joy that humdrum days withheld.
I was a joy lifting a scrap from the rag-rug.
No staircase since then
has led to a leaner paradise.

Removal vans drew children like ambulances.
Everything looked poorer in the merciless light.
The flower-pots like a final greeting to the
                    obsequies of intimacies,
beds, bedclothes, contorted chairs:
everything crouched under a shroud that came too late.
We were caught out! But we discovered things too:
empty rooms where we'd lived, grease-spots behind the tapestry
and the scratched floors, the gas-cooker rusting away.
Deprived of a room the spirit crouched, given
over to shoddy things whose warmth no-one could see.
I jolted along on the front of the load, I was
born a lodger.

Spring was mostly a biting wind.
In the park where the bottles sprang out
                      when the black snow melted
old leaves blew around.

Mother only mentioned her a couple of times.
There wasn't much to say.
She lived alone after her husband and only son
drowned one July night off Högholmen.
She greeted us silenty and silently we responded.
She was the only one who hung a Christmas wreath
                    of whortleberry sprigs on her door.
The third Christmas it hung there late into January,
and there was no sign of her.
Mother suspected something.
They found her, but didn't let me see.
Everything was all clean and tidy, said Mother to Father,
as if she'd been expecting a visitor.

There was a tree in the inner courtyard.
It stood there anxiously most of the time.
On windy spring days its last year's leaves still
                              rustled along the walls.
Now when I see it rather more as a tree
than the upright broom we took it for
I'm writing a tardy but deeply-felt poem in its honour:

    Autumn leaves
    under the bright
    spring branches –

The house slowly put out new rooms into the darkness,
new passages and staircases, a courtyard behind the
                    courtyard,
closed doors there – hush! – someone called, plaintively,
or was it just imagination, shadows, misunderstanding?

At the same time the house slowly shrank, the walls
                    closed in,
took on the colour of skin, the colour of tired
                    eyes when they saw
blotches spread over the ceiling, as if someone
was bleeding through the floor, but no sound was heard.

Slowly we grew older and ran up and down stairs
that echoed without response through hot summer days.
Evenings darkened, filled with windows and lamps.

'How does he manage on what he's got? He's got
                    next to nothing,
anyway nothing worth mentioning, a bed, a table,
and food – you know how it is when a lonely man –
my old Dad was like that too, well, we let him,
                    he just got thin,
almost transparent, prematurely yellow – not that he'd
                    say anything to you,
even though I always looked him straight in the eye:
                    someone who won't look at you,
I tell you, maybe he's avoiding something else as well!'

'Maybe he's avoiding life – or he's proud – '

'Proud? Who can afford to be that? Just as
you can't afford not to live.
And there's no time to be so uppity either.'

The elderly man in a room with kitchenette
has cuffs black with Indian ink.
He walks with a silver-handled cane
and tries to keep poverty
within civilised limits.
He's on the defensive as if he had
a constant observer.

In the November dark the water is no longer water,
it moves cold and sluggish like black oil
                    sprinkled with broken light.
It will never be summer again.

Not one of them was a reader. Mother read.
And I followed, lost to the outside world.

Far from not telling dream from seen
you learn to see.

You learn to be ready for catastrophes, too,
it feels like a sickness.

What people see as flight may perhaps
                be readiness.

There was hardly anyone who didn't keep a secret
from somebody.
It was a condition of life: that it could be lived
in spite of the days.
Only the old folk leaned their bodies
wearily against each other, as if they'd
                    been grazing in the same meadow.
We had gardens that climbed out of every crack,
we hid their fruits in every unseen corner.
We taught ourselves caution early,
we taught ourselves the plunderer's grasp.
You could even make yourself invisible
if you held your breath.

As when nearing a station
one morning when the sun breaks through smoke
and the tangle of lines unravels,
the rumble fades from the tracks, I wait –

As when someone turns their sick face towards me
and I wait, the cold round lamps in the ward
form a distant mute pattern
and the hand is frail, already almost dead –

and both these feelings mix, it's bearable
like the heaviest, loneliest thing
you felt as a child, grew up with and knew.

I woke to someone screaming in the courtyard.
I woke to a smell of gas: they were all dead, me too.

I woke to the outbreak of war and my clothes burning.
There was utter silence. Only Father snored comfortingly.

I woke to so many catastrophes –
In training for the future.

One summer I went to camp.
We slept in a row on iron beds.
Mother worried but it was something
we both had to cope with.
It was green everywhere and we had school food.
A railway ran close by.
We stood and watched the trains go past
now this way, now that.

You had to watch out not to step on lines, spit at cats,
walk under ladders, run upstairs two at a time
till you were panting after release from self-imposed
                    torture.
The kitchen tablecloth had its maddening pattern.
There were always rules. The exceptions were like
                    summer swallows,
rare sweeping cries soon gone
and the courtyard quiet as Sunday.
The rules were there to make life more secret
                    than it was.
And thoughts moved hushed as a shuttle
and wove the most intricate webs
or wondrous colours.

We fell headlong into savage ambush, stood up,
killed when it was our turn, fired in a frenzy.
We leapt through silences, streets and houses,
or crept breathlessly on towards the dark,
broke up late, came in late and sat down under
                    the table-lamp,
and to the question, 'Where have you been so long?'
we answered: 'Nowhere. Why?' or sat silent.

I never saw my own roof.
It was like others: swaying black chimneys,
tiles like gore that stretched
hardened arteries down along the murmuring house.
The wind in the attic went echoing through a framework
of wires.
The smell of old cloth, of burning – had there been a fire? –
hung silently round discarded furniture, piles of
newspapers,
skiis, bicycles; or almost empty compartments,
prisons of filtering light.
Underneath lived the lektor with velvet curtains
who could see the sea.

The distance from her was like an evening twilight.

Come in and see me. No, you needn't be afraid.
You're helpless if you've lived alone as long as I have.
Most of the time I sit here watching you all
                    play in the courtyard.
If I didn't have a son who sent me money then . . .
                    I don't know.
Perhaps it would be just as well. When you seldom
have anyone to talk to you start to wonder.
Sit you down. You can have a cup of coffee, and needn't
stay long. D'you know, I've watched you growing up
ever since you were so high. Help yourself. What I
                    was going to say
was: when you're left on your own
you somehow stop living, it's as if you'd been scrubbed.
You bleed away, then just go on sitting here.
Money helps you stay alive and yet
it doesn't help. With that . . . Am I boring you?
I'm so used to chattering on to myself
I don't seem able to talk to anyone. Not properly.
It's as if this courtyard's not here anymore.
There was a time when I used to read, but my eyes aren't
                    up to it now.
How old are you? Ten? Just as well.
I don't suppose you understand what I'm on about.
Just you run along when you like. And come back – some
                    time.
If you feel like it. Go on then, off with you.

Underneath him lived yet another who couldn't stand
children:
                              face red as a September moon
he drove off every day to his shipping agency
from a terror-struck home.
Underneath him again lived the Lehtonens with their
                              seven children,
all in trade. They were like ants.
Underneath them lived the four of us,
there was sunshine in the living-room between 11 and 12.
Underneath us were the dark caverns that swallow up
                              every living thing
and where I sometimes stood as if the whole house
was slowly falling on top of me floor by floor.
It wouldn't have surprised me
if the hollow floor had been stuffed with human hair,
or blood had come spurting from the snaking waterpipes.

She looked over her shoulder as she stood bent over
the wash-tub
with water dripping from the half wrung-out shirt:
was that someone banging a door, wasn't she alone?
She must be mistaken.
Suddenly she saw her hands' mechanical movement:
long bony fingers, swollen knotted joints, red-patched
and soapy.
She had to sit down on the wooden bench and lean
against the copper.
It was as if the dingy light grew even weaker.

After exactly an hour he got up.
Life returned to space and sound.
When they talked I was alone again.
Everything was light when darkness passed.

He must have thought: I've had enough.
He walked towards the door but the door came towards him.
It struck him hard, stayed locked.
He hit it so the staircase shook.
But the door forced him towards the bedroom wall
where the family slept.
The door forced him into the wall, it grew like a mark
that doesn't go away.
Head bowed into a corner, arms at an angle:
he was back in the room.
When he grew numb the door opened.
The dark came streaming in.
He could no longer go out.

Silence, it's the silence after those who could
                        form nothing in words,
who could not point at the rivulet, say: it's my blood,
I'm not alive, I'm dying.
Silence, it's the step that's broken by doors
                                    that are locked
and the open eyes there,
all that stayed unsaid like ice between them
who perhaps had once kept faith –
there's no silence to hear in silence, no song,
no-one listens to the rain.
There's nothing unsaid, there's nothing to talk about,
there is the courtyard, there the old folk, there the
                        sleepers, there the children, there:
the children are silent, too, lie in rows.
If they knew they couldn't speak,
would they at last speak?

Children are so small you can run over them
Or stick pointed hats on them and give them
a wand with a star, make them sing shrilly in chorus
in a playroom with tiny chairs and concertinaed socks
over by Sörnäs Square.
Children are so small you can jerk them by the arm
and sew it on again firmly if it loosens and then
put them in a corner
or make them jump round and round in a courtyard
till some fall down, or line them up in a row
and then squeeze them into the cold lysol of primary school.
In the dark you can light their eyes
till they shine like flashlights or flames!

For a moment they stand out but mostly they're faceless.
They wear a peaked cap and a hard shadow or narrow legs
that take them out into the street and on past dizzy heights
down to the sea and the Russian church and the houses
                    where only the dead live.
They're sprinkled like seed and buried among old houses
and come up gasping for air in the dark where a few lamps
rock and strike against patterned plaster walls with black iron.
There pale girls grab them, tough as their voices,
have swarms of children and move with big mattresses
to smaller rooms where coughs and joblessness live snug.
On early misty mornings when spring rises from the sea
and the children have stormed from the nest they sit with
                    long still hands
and watch us playing, if they see us at all, they're buried
in wear and tear, overlong raincoats, their stubble
                    silver-white.
Later they're just not there.
They probably lived in the same place for forty years,
and walked along streets and in through dark portals
where suddenly no one was in.
Those days when they're borne away are always in mind
shrouded in chimney smoke.

Like sitting in a hotel lounge in a provincial town
in a totally strange country and looking out of
                    the window:
a square empty of people, falling rain, the long wait
in the same lifeless room, and thinking: What brought
                    me here?
Why am I miles from home?
What's the idea, why did I pick this place?
As if to see how inescapable, coincidental it is.
And through the rain see someone walking alone and
                    vanishing, pushing a cycle,
and wanting to follow them – speak – no, sit
in solitude and recall how it once was, the low windows
on the courtyard, the rain, no one home,
any more, ever.

from
The Spring
(1973)

The dream

Then in the dream you looked at me.
Others were there, we were having coffee.
From some adjoining room light shone
into the vague feeling: I'm dreaming.
There you sat, dark hair combed back.
Calm mouth, troubled eyes, wrinkled: close.
As if I hadn't seen you before
I turned to my uncle who
was chatting to someone on my left.
'But I thought she'd died,' I said.
He stopped talking, turned to me:
'Didn't you know?'

They are alive

They are alive,
here
as long as you remember them,

at a distance,
shrouded,
saying something –

they're walking behind the hedge,
you almost reach them
or the wind,

pale, like linen.

In the blind alley

She said I was to wait here.
I've been waiting a long time and think
something has happened to her.
If you stand in the dark with gaze turned inward,
no stars, no light,
and hear only your own blood nailing you to earth
as if you were a cripple –
then perhaps a longer wait, a kind of chill
is what steadies you so you don't quite fall apart.
Deep enough inside
you learn to see the wall that's before you.
And the darkness merely wind and nothingness.
Like litter blown along the street and away.

In the north

I have no breakthtaking view over valley and mountain.
The few flowers that bloom, bloom late, and the grass
is patchy, pushes bravely up through the clay in June.
That southern beauty I accept and give away again
like a wonderful object, almost weightless.
The abyss drops down here quite imperceptibly,
right through grey days, mist of little landscapes.
Sometimes I get dizzy at very low heights
as in a film with angst like Harold Lloyd's
perspective is all, and chiefly what it excludes.
What you don't see sharpens the eye and the feelings
and most rowanberries are both bitter and lovely.

Out of the trap

So once again I've scrabbled my way out of a trap.
Digging pits in yourself is a long-term job.
Self-discipline! Sooner or later
we're all tabbed in a zoo.
You have to dig yourself out before that,
some night, alone with wine and moon:
not even the old Chinese had need
of anything else.
What's important is to pass
unnoticed through history.

The little poem

Someone was always talking about the little poem.
It was seen to fly cheeping
up, up on frail wings to the rosy clouds –
a budgie no doubt.
It wasn't easy to catch up with, its voice a mere hole
                    marked
like a needle-prick in that web of things seen and held
                    in memory
swaddling house and home.
But a hole is a hole.
Close enough to us it could block out the sun
with a shadow that struck our face like a hard wing
so we suddenly looked our dread in the face.
But as I said: little birds are little birds.
Much depends on mobility.

Life was given me

Life was given me one morning in a snowstorm.
Cloths and bundles torn from the hands of the poor.
There was no horizon out over the sea.

On gramophones fragrant with foreign cities
Patti and the Charleston screeched through scratchy
needles.
Tin roofs swelled with fruit and split,

out poured shabby bonnets, cane prams,
were sliced by jolting trams,
snow piled round the high misted windows.

Life was given me where others threw it from them.
bodies that no-one saw, merely felt in the dark.
Those died: they knew all about the living,

but of the dead the living knew nothing.

There had been sunlight in the gardens

I walked through the damp narrow streets.
There had been sunlight in the gardens.
It was darkest halfway along where I shrank
silent against the walls
trying to squeeze into them so as
                      not to be seen.
Metal drainpipes, damp mortar – and there

the sea crystal–clear between houses,
a light meeting the eye,
a poverty's longing
revealed.

With days

With days I have flooded
my life, with days,
with days,

with heavy days
carried away,
unseen,

with towns I have filled each hour,
with towns,
with their echoes,

and rested without rest,
yes, without rest.

The spring

Far across the fields
sounds, faint but clear
the vernal spring.
I listen,
try to get closer.

The water echoes, rippling
through fresh,
sun-scented summer forests.
I go on my way,
searching.

Already plain
among autumn treetops
is the long valley
where a hidden
stream murmurs. I must rest.

As if snow were in the air,
endless as our footsteps.
I listen, it's close.
The voice of the spring, fainter,
still there,
invisible.

from
In Dark Rooms
In Light Rooms
(1976)

From a hilltop I see a wide sea
beneath a dark cloud-bank,

an ever-changing surface,
moving yet unmoving –

this surface utterly clear against the dark,
the waves' murmuring close yet still,

and beneath this flux, darkness,
silence and cold.

The door opened on to the garden.
Tools lay around, abandoned since autumn.
Light fell through the birches and from the road
came a faint rumble that replaced the wind.

I stood there alone with my eyes.
The earth was ice-bound, uneven,
the clouds rushed swiftly past
as cars pass an unknown town, with
                    rain-slashed windows.

Before sleep brightens
the landscape comes nearer through falling snow,
you dream you're awake
it's dark in a room without walls,

before you grow old
and see in memory the forest
and the roads that ended.
Dreaming the darkness is water,

still moving around you
like a touch, and speaking
with voices – so many voices
in the lonely winter night.

You wake and it's quiet.
You hear sounds but the world is dumb
as the darkness, and the roads are empty,
passable.

I saw a tree
outside the tree,

it stood in its shadow
with a dark crown,

image laid on image,
the trunk rough

like a scent, a freshness
in reality.

The earth gives out solemnity
because it hides so many dead.
The meadow's so lovely, its beauty so light.
The solemn roots make the crown bright.

The cauliflower is a hard cloud,
a brain substance,
each floret part of the stem.
It grows unseen,
hidden in green leaves,
then swells,
with a spatter of earth,
a faint scent of poison
as if eyes were blind
or filled with tears
but aren't.

Someone has gone out of the room
and left their clothes behind.
What's happening?

Someone didn't manage to shut the door.
Whatever was carried out was heavy
like the sofa, the table, the bed.

Now everything's tidy, I think.
And the air is fresher
when the window's open.

When you drive up to the four-star pump
there's always another car, grubby, empty,
just standing there, God knows where its owner is.
The registration number shows he's a local.
By the self-service pump: no-one.
It's dirty and cold, strip lighting here too,
and a deafening drill blocks your ears,
digs a pit for a new tank.

At the cash point you can buy
sweets, cassettes, porn mags, condoms
and, tanked up, oil-filled, with a clean windscreen
drive out into the dark landscape
before one of the gang hanging round outside
grabs hold of the door and staggering, with a face
pale as paper, yells something
you can't catch, which scares you
or fills you with rage, later
when you're alone on the road, and the radio's
playing wonderful clear Vivaldi.

I am no lamp shining in darkening corridors:
I am the darkening corridors.

You are no window opening for runners through
                    passages:
you are the passages.

We are not the house floating in the air beneath bridges,
we are house, air and bridges,

we are the room, the passages, the house
that's now a city.

In frosty fields, in a stag's voice in the mist
are springtime light, lark's song.

In the reed's dry light, in morning ice
are the frail shadows of violet

that herald the birch's bright crown.
In each thesis is an airy antithesis,

and in the seen, to be seen as a child
sees through the lens of joy

are dreams, fragile leaves
in the still dark winter depths.

The horned owl, suddenly there
at dusk.
It glides into the thicket
like a moment's heartbeat.
Suddenly it turns
its wide gaze,
wraps itself in shadow.
The small birds
mere shadows too.
Later it glides quietly off
followed by angry screams
till the heart opens again
to the summer night.

You walk up a path to the table
with a blank sheet of paper.
Soon the night's north wind
will blow away, hurry!
There's fruit on the table,
flowers in plain glass jars, and,
                    among the trees,
people who turn and smile.
There the Camberwell Beauty flaps
up into the old oak,
folds its wings and fades from sight
against the dizzy sky.
At the table you see
paper filled with writing,
you sit down, lean your head
against the cool table-top.
There's a glass of spring water,
                        the tall grass
hums with bees,
and grasshoppers signal.
All the wooded slope sparkles
after the thunder-storm,
As in dream or waking,
a sleep, a poem
under closed eyelids, senses open
like clouds.

As I've said, I didn't know what use
this raindrop with its pearls
was to me, then, in childhood.

And now? See it resembles a trace,
a memory of how I stood then,
and watched the rain.

It isn't time that changes us,
it's space: the forest low as a dark ribbon
round the evening when we were children.
And the water that reached our feet.

It's the road that's straightened out,
the same trees, houses, people
looking out of the windows
that are windows in space, not in time.

Room for children, room for the lovers
where birds fly in and out,
room for the one who sleeps so light
not even death's breath is heard.

The furniture in the room's the same,
the same branches in front of it
as if the room were your gaze —
that never ends.

from
The Day is Turning
(1983)

The day is turning

1

The day is turning.
He's getting up
above the living.
He sees, early,
how the growing things of spring
know nothing of autumn's power,
of decaying bark,
wormy dust,
the indifferent tramping feet,
the blood on the beach.
Why then don't they see
the harelip behind the fir tree
or the consumptive
just by the curtains
in the nursery,
the burned, torn down?
He rises, walks,
takes a journey from himself,
sees his skin, white and cool,
rubbing the wet window.
Mist and moonlight.
Now none of the dead
venture from their graves,
lie in wet clay,
sink deeper and deeper into it
with their backbent heads.
They are the confirmation,
the pause in the conversation,
they regard him:
Where are you going?
Who are you going to meet?
But they say nothing,
sink into the dim lamps,
their faces are flattened out
but they don't know it.
The world is sinking
but they don't know it.

The day is turning,
he strolls down the stairs,
hesitates, throws open the door,
is hurled into dumbness,
into the winds,
into the thin breath of the dead,
their unheard lamenting.

2

The day is turning,
the instant shatters,
the wall does not yield to the cry,
the cry flies winged
over the hard roofs
among shining clouds.
Then there is silence again,
there is peace in the shadows
there, round the courtyard tree.
The woman passing by
stops, struck by
some memory –
But in the secret corridors
the wind bides
with sand and dust,
ashes and remnants.
Suddenly the child opens
the door to the courtyard:
the wind lurks, an animal
quiet, stealthy,
it's already dusk.
A chill rises
as if stones were water,
the day is turning,
something is broken, snapped,
that only the child sees:
there's the taste of blood on the tongue
as if frozen fast to metal,
pain you can imagine,

the tearing – a part of the city,
flakes of soot flashing
as from an invisible stove,
whirling upwards,
meeting the snow
that's starting to fall –

Time stops, goes, stops
like a worn-out heart,
the day is turning,
the dead stand solemnly
hidden in the darkness:
Have you learned nothing?
Haven't you been warned?
They fade, they pale,
in the gateway
the girl with dark hair
is glimpsed, vanishes –
is she calling?
The child grows,
goes seeking
beside the yielding foundations,
here was a house
that could fly,
shadows and summers,
over the streets
rumbles a skeleton car
heavier than bone and stone,
something is given painful birth
with neck bent back,
longs for peace, kills peace.
Metal casks rumble,
huge heavy churns, full of blood,
he dreams of them,
how every wound stays open,
how the rain dissolves everything,
stone destroys bone, metal destroys stone,
the snow falls for no one,
the day for no one,
time stands stony as the dead
and cannot die deeper –

Then he cries
through the silence,
cries: I am alive!
I am here!
Someone is tracking me down!
Someone. He sees:
someone pulling a cart,
there are old crosses,
distorted, mouldering,
junk, bits of weapons,
glittering, burning,
torn-off limbs
sinking into the ground,
flakes are hurled against
black asphalt –

The day is turning,
it's November,
there's a faint wailing,
a common sorrow,
a whirring note,
it drives him
up against the wall:
there it still stands,
the spring tree, the guardian tree,
with leaves like flames,
the snow whirls round
like a circle of longing,
there's a light
like a summer night lamp,
the day is turning,
it falls, he falls,
the ground catches him,
the silence closes over him,
he sees, he knows:
if I can see this, I am saved,
hollows and bones of the face,
the cry the door cut off,
the echo that shakes
the ice-cold staircase,
the threat that's slowly torn down
as a house is torn,

stone by stone,
hour by hour,
there's no stillness,
cries fly with wings,
walls give way,
the instant breaks into the eye
like a knife:
air is burning!
With every moment
the darkness falls ever faster,
wind carries with it
heavy waves of mire.
He stands a moment more,
head held high,
with closed eyes,
two flakes
on his eyelids.

3

The day is turning,
streets empty of life,
it is sucked up
by the descending darkness,
in every thing
a maggot, a dust of death –

the child dies
in the adult,
the sun is covered with cloud
as the wound
with stained cotton
that sucks up the blood –

the day is turning,
a barely heard lamenting
as if the ground lamented,
the asphalt, the walls
and the mouldering parks
arise out of human decay:
each stone, each trunk,

the abode of longing
slowly sinking,
bent on death
like the black mother
beside husband and child –

the day is falling,
casts its iron band
around houses and courtyards
in faint lantern-light,
the mute language
begins to live
like signs in stone,
slowly emerges,
shadowed, blackened –

lights are lit,
with its hand
the child shadows the adults
falling backward
into sleep,
dreams move there,
light-traces, splinters
and flying houses
with floors of water –

soon all has gone,
only the sleepers
talk with the snow
streaming, streaming
into oblivion –

the day is turning,
the day is falling,
as a light-ray falls
in dreams, the dead fall
smiling towards us,

welcoming,
blessing,
with their thin
frail limbs.

In that house

In that house dusk came like a blanket
with the sheet shining over its edge.
The white courtyard wore a pattern of footprints
as if voices had lingered there
and listened to the lanterns' fifteen-watt bulbs.
In that house the pigeons sat silent,
stared nervously over the roof where the smoke
went wreathing like ribbon around the moon.

In that house you heard footsteps before folk were
                                     awake,
their dreams rang with the clatter of buckets
and low voices hovered around the child
who lay feigning sleep.
Like the plaster, something was always crumbling
and the sudden gusts bumped drunkenly
against the iron-shod wooden stairs.
In that house was mortar for every future house.

Heaven and earth

You remember the morning
when you were made to eat the porridge
and the nicotine-marked thumb
that rubbed salt on the stain

you remember the room
that hugged its own darkness
and the luminous snow
that fell inside you

you remember the door that slammed
through the silence of staircase C
something in you observes the heavens
and something heavier, earth

The old ones

We met them on the way down,
the old ones

weary despite coolness and shade
as if they'd asked forgiveness
or not dared to ask

eyes to the ground
afraid of falling
into the heavens

Santa Claus

Santa Claus peers out through beard and spruce
to ask if there are any good children here.

The grown-ups laugh, they aren't children,
Santa Claus doesn't ask them if they're good,

they can get up if they want to, scream and knock
                    down the Christmas tree,
set fire to the whole room,

and Santa will demand nothing, nothing.

Old man

He turns his life inwards to the courtyard.
                    It is dark.
He was born in the century that blew away
and sees how something forgotten
rises and falls like waves of asphalt.
The sunlight strikes him like a blow.
Someone braced his foot against a breast
and pulled out the bayonet, blood came streaming
warm, thick, like oil.
It darkened before his eyes and stayed there,
the men lay on the scorched slope,
swallows whooped over the roof, their screams swift
                    as shadows.
Twenty years old, overgrown, the second birth,
the woman's averted eyes
forced him into himself, just as he
forced himself into her.
The rest was work, poverty, stone
as long as stone was needed.
So people fade, die,
The years rose in him, like marsh water.
The third birth: into the silence, the backyard Sunday,
unreal, waiting, a wisp of smoke,
unseen.

Cycle

Then they rise from the table
and go out through us and away

and leave the candle on the table
for us to bend over and blow out

till only pale light from snow
is left behind the empty windows.

Memory

Inside the doorway are
torn-out pictures – a memory
like something left over,

a dark negative, finally developed
on the day I leave –

the memory is that part of the present
which exposes the future.

The city

The city a growing shadow on the plain, sunlit.
First some temples dedicated to the gods,
later down the years winding roads and arches,
squares resting in quiet, flaming at morning,
river-mists beside damp walls, bridges
black with people;

the murmur of water or of voices, rising,
in the sacred groves cries of birds and children,
from within the town's teeming streets, tottering houses,
and at night moonlight and silence.
Only soft as a plea the dying
river's song and breath.

A shudder; a muddy shore-line that sinks
into the rippling vapours. But at morning
the children play again in the clear, cool air.
In strong wind under bridges you can see
the dark river bed, dim bubbles of gas,
and hear echoes from the yawning chasm.

Slowly at night the mist of terror advances,
each cry in sleep is the earth shuddering
but in daylight human murmurings rise
on wings, happy, with black streaks.
Yet sometimes from the bridges, gaping holes
open on to the depths;

then the years rise, fall nearer the abyss,
leafy groves wither while a strange lament
breaks out among those sleepers,
in the room near the deep precipices.
Plunge! Cry the half-dream-drowned,
the death-ridden, while still at evening the air

fills with the scent of flowers or at morning
fresh-baked bread. And those who still see
                          and hear the beauty
for a moment hold city, plain and firmament together,
death's hounds are held at bay and in the silence
a child's voice sounds like a flower out of the light,
a warning, a sign.